# Shoes Through the Ages

## Written by Marlene Targ Brill

**STECK-VAUGHN**
ELEMENTARY · SECONDARY · ADULT · LIBRARY

A Harcourt Classroom Education Company

www.steck-vaughn.com

# Contents

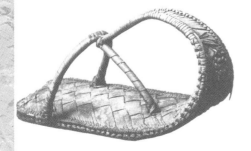

# Chapter 1

# Stepping Out

**D**id you know that most people take about 4,000 steps each day? At that rate, a person will walk around the world more than 2 times by age 75. Can you imagine walking that far without wearing shoes?

People of today step out in many different kinds of shoes. We wear everyday shoes and dress shoes. We wear work shoes and shoes for almost every kind of sport. We have slip-on shoes, lace-up shoes, shoes with low heels, and shoes with high heels. But no matter what kind of shoes we choose, the main reason we wear them is to protect our feet.

Most kinds of shoes have two important parts. The **sole** is the bottom of a shoe. It lies under the feet. Soles are made to last through months of walking, running, and playing. Some soles have many layers. Many have heels. Both can make shoes stronger.

The **upper** is the top part of a shoe. It gives the shoe its shape. Uppers that go up to the ankle create shoes. Shoes with uppers that reach higher than the ankle are called boots. Shoes with uppers made of straps are called sandals.

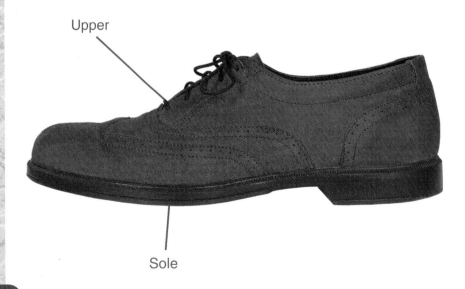

Upper

Sole

# Chapter 2

# Early Shoes

Who wore the first shoes? What were the first shoes like? Many shoe facts are still a mystery. But people who study the past think that the earliest foot coverings were animal skins wrapped around the feet. These shoes were like socks because they had no soles. They were made by Stone Age (until about 4000 B.C.) people living in very cold places. Skin socks kept the feet warm. Some Stone Age people stuffed dried grass into their skin socks. The grass helped keep their feet dry as well as warm.

Not long ago hikers in Italy found a 5,000-year-old mummy. They called him the Ice Man. This **ancient** man wore calfskin socks lined with grass to warm his feet.

The Ice Man used strings to hold his skin socks in place.

Skin socks were fine for people in cold lands. But what about people in warm places? They wore sandals, of course. Sandals were the first true shoes. Why? Skin socks were really only animal skins wrapped around the feet. Sandals had an upper and a sole. People needed to plan how to make them and what to make them from. They also had to spend time and energy to create them.

The oldest sandals found so far were uncovered in a North American cave. Scientists believe that the shoes are about 10,000 years old. Grass and shredded bark form the sole. Grass and twisted ropes form the upper. Rabbit fur and pine needles pad the sole for comfort.

The world's oldest sandals

Many early people wore sandals. Some groups of people wore them to show wealth and power. One picture from ancient Egypt shows a king and other people in a battle. None of the people are wearing shoes. Yet a servant follows behind, carrying a pair of sandals for the king. The sandals and the servant to carry them show that the king has great power.

Egyptian kings and queens wore sandals.

Egypt's rich people, priests, and warriors also wore sandals. They hired shoemakers to make the shoes out of leather and plant leaves. The shoemakers sometimes decorated the shoes with designs, picture writing, and gold ribbon. One ancient sandal from Egypt left footprints that said "Follow me." Sandals were so important in Egypt that they were buried with their dead owners. The owners believed they would wear the sandals in a later life.

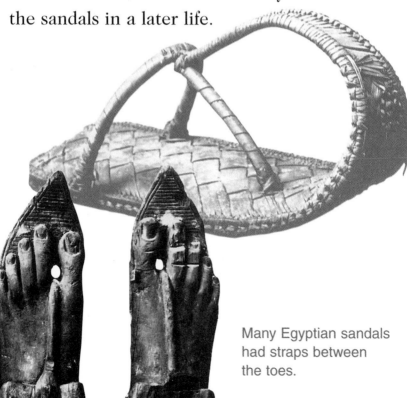

Many Egyptian sandals had straps between the toes.

Ancient Greeks and Romans made shoes a form of fashion. Warriors brought back new styles from lands they had conquered. Some sandals tied around the ankle. Others had open toes or a strap between two toes to form a **thong**.

Rich Greek women thought nothing of owning 10 or 20 pairs of shoes, mostly sandals. Some women wore sandals with flaps that folded over the straps and upper foot. The flaps often shone with gold or silver or with detailed designs.

This Greek woman wears sandals with thick soles.

Sometimes Greek slaves wore shoes, but only on long trips away from home. They almost never wore shoes where they lived because wearing shoes meant that a person was free. For the same reason, wealthy Greeks made sure they wore shoes. They feared others might think they were slaves if they went without shoes.

Rome later conquered Greece, but the Romans kept Greek shoe styles. The Romans did add their own ideas about color, though. Then anyone could judge the power and wealth of others by the color of their shoes.

One Roman ruler wore purple sandals that glittered with gold thread. A gold eagle perched on the front of each shoe. Only the ruler could wear these purple sandals. Anyone else seen wearing shoes like them was banned from the country. On special days the rest of the royal household wore purple boots.

Senators often wore red shoes. Other rich men wore black ones. Farmers and poor people covered their feet with fitted leather shoes or low boots of a natural color.

Soldiers wore plain leather boots with open toes. Their boots also had iron nails stuck into the soles. The nails helped the shoes last longer, and they gripped roads better. Can you imagine an army of Roman soldiers running down a road? They must have rumbled like thunder. What a scary sound to an enemy!

Many Roman sandals had ankle straps.

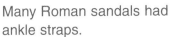

People in the Roman Empire were not the only ones making shoes during this time. On the other side of the globe, several Native American groups were making **moccasins**. Many groups took special pride in their moccasins. Some made the shoes from soft deerskin. Some attached beaver quills dyed with purple berries and yellow clay for decoration. Traders exchanged moccasins for food and other goods. The most beautiful moccasins became gifts to friends.

Some Native Americans used colorful beads to decorate their moccasins.

Many Europeans who later settled in North America liked wearing moccasins. Some sent moccasins home to Europe. Moccasins became North America's first shoe style.

# Chapter 3

# Shoe Fashions

Sandals for everyday wear began to disappear after the Roman Empire ended. People began to cover their body with more clothing than in the past. They began to cover up more of their feet, too. The most popular foot coverings were shoes with soft soles. Most were made from natural, untreated leather. These shoes slipped over the foot and pointed slightly at the toe.

Styles from Asia sparked ideas for interesting shoe materials. Satin and velvet cloth, buckles, and lace were attached to the front and sides of shoes. Shoe artists painted or cut designs on shoes for the rich.

Most Asian shoes were made of cloth because those countries had little leather.

A pair of French sabots

During this time people in Europe began to wear handmade wooden shoes. They were sturdy and easy to care for. In these solid shoes, workers could plod through soggy farmland, mines, and stone pits. They could tramp over wet docks and into muddy mills without getting soggy feet.

Names for wooden shoes were different in each country. The English called them **clogs**, meaning "lumps of wood." To the Dutch they were *klompen* (KLAHMP uhn). The French called them *sabots* (sah BOHZ). In one French tale, unhappy factory workers threw their sabots into the machines. The shoes shut down the machines, so the factories were forced to close. From these events came the word *sabotage*. *Sabotage* means "an action that is meant to destroy or hurt."

Wooden shoes played an important part on some special days. On December 5, St. Nicholas

Eve, Dutch children left their wooden shoes by the fireplace at night. They placed a poem inside the shoe for the kindly saint. They filled the shoe with hay and a carrot for his white horse. The children hoped that St. Nicholas would come during the night and fill their shoes with treats.

Shoes added to celebrations in other parts of the world, too. Early settlers in England started a new wedding custom. A bride threw a shoe to her bridesmaids. The bridesmaid who caught the shoe was supposed to marry next. Brides today throw flowers after their wedding in much the same way. Some newlyweds drive away from their wedding with shoes tied behind their car!

Many modern clogs have carving on them.

In the 1300s pointy-toed shoes became very popular in Europe. Most people called them **crakows** (KRAH kowz) because they began in the city of Krakow, Poland.

Crakows were shoes for the wealthy. In fact, the longer the pointy toe, the wealthier the owner. Crakows became so long that their toes had to be stuffed with wool, hay, or whalebone to keep them stiff. The toes of some shoes extended almost 2 feet (60 centimeters). That was far beyond the end of the foot. Some crakows had silver bells that jingled at the end of their turned-up toe.

Walking in crakows was hard. Working in them was even harder. Rich men everywhere had to shuffle around in their flapping shoes. Many men found the long points so clumsy that they tied them to thin chains. They attached the chains to knee bands. Can you imagine walking in such a get-up?

A leather crakow from the 1400s

Servants of rich people also wore crakows.

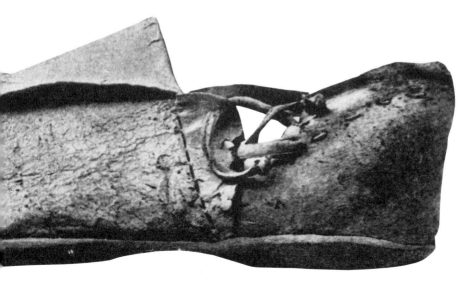

The king of England wanted to make sure that only wealthy men wore crakows. He passed the first laws on how long the toes of someone's shoes could be. Common people had to be happy with only 6-inch (15-centimeter) points. Rich nobles could have 24-inch (60-centimeter) points on their crakows.

Later laws were more strict. One law ordered shoemakers to stop making shoes with long toes for common people. Shoemakers had to pay a fine if they broke this law. France totally outlawed long points in 1470. Still, long-toed shoes stayed trendy in Europe for some time.

Some men slipped their limp crakows into thicker shoes called **pattens**. These overshoes of rugged iron or wood protected the dainty crakows.

Pattens raised long, pointy shoes high enough off the ground to keep them clean and dry.

Women of the 1400s wore tall, heavy hats and long gowns.

Women of this time stayed clear of extra-long shoes. They wore shoes with pointy toes, but their points were usually not as long as the men's. Back then women had enough trouble walking in all the other things they wore.

Many shoe fads began with kings and queens. The more unusual the style, the more eager they and other wealthy people were to wear them. After long-toed shoes went out of style, shoes with wide toes popped up. Some say that England's King Henry VIII started this trend. He began wearing wide-toed **slippers** to ease his foot problems. The style caught on with men and some women, but they carried the trend too far. Shoe toes grew wider and wider until some toes spread up to 12 inches (30 centimeters) across. People gave the shoes the nicknames "duck bills" and "bear paws."

Henry VIII of England in a pair of duck bills

Shoemakers went crazy with wide-toed designs. They lowered shoe sides and backs. They stuffed and rolled the toes of the shoes to make them giant-size. They sliced the leather to spread out the toe even wider. Under the openings they sewed fabric that matched the clothing that they wore. The fabric puffed through the slits.

Baggy shoes were stylish, but they were not very useful. Once again people turned to pattens to protect their shoes and help them walk.

A German duck bill from the 1500s

A new, thicker kind of patten called the **chopine** (shoh PEEN) became popular during the 1500s. Chopines were first worn in Turkey. Women there wanted to keep their feet and skirts off muddy ground. Turkish chopines looked like stubby wooden stilts.

Traders brought the chopine style to Italy. Chopines then became a great fad in Europe. Soon huge platforms lifted women up as much as 18 inches (45 centimeters) off the ground. Soft slippers sat on top of these perches.

Rich women of this time liked chopines because they made women taller. The women also liked the fancy paint, cloth, gold thread, and stones that decorated chopines. But women walked as if they were on tall tin cans. Chopines limited where women could go and what they could do. Many women needed servants to help them walk in these clumsy shoes. Otherwise they would trip and fall.

A chopine had two parts—the platform and the slipper. ⟶

Shoes with high heels that women wear today developed from pattens and chopines. Some people think that the newer styles began with a rich woman from Italy in the 1500s. This woman wanted shoes that made her as tall as her new

This Italian woman may have worn the first high heels.

husband. That way, she could look at him eye-to-eye. She also wanted to walk without tripping. Her shoemaker created thick cork wedges that raised her shoes higher in the back.

A high-heeled shoe from the 1600s

At first most heels on women's shoes were made of cork or wood. These early heels rose about 3 to 5 inches ($7\frac{1}{2}$ to $12\frac{1}{2}$ centimeters), and they were rather thick. With time heel shapes became smaller and thinner.

Modern high-heeled shoes

Today many women refuse to wear shoes with high heels—and for good reason. Even the lower ones can cause foot problems for women. High heels push many of the 26 bones in the foot forward. Only a few tiny bones are left to support the entire body. Young girls can develop foot and back problems later in life because of high heels.

Shoe customs caused great pain for many young girls in China. About 200 years ago, lily foot slippers were a mark of wealth and beauty. These fancy cloth slippers had beautiful threads sewn into bird and flower shapes.

But lily foot slippers had to be an ideal size. They had to be tiny. A perfect lily foot measured only 4 inches (10 centimeters) long, a size that fit into the palm of the hand. To fit into the small slippers, girls' feet were bound. Foot-binding started when girls were about 5 years old. Mothers wrapped long bandages tightly around the girls' feet. The four smaller toes were bent under the foot. The feet were bound until the bones in the feet stopped growing.

Foot-binding was painful for young girls. It also kept them from running and jumping. Foot-binding prevented older women from doing hard work. Women with bound feet shuffled around with very tiny steps. Even with these problems, Chinese people believed that small feet improved a woman's chances of marrying well.

A Chinese woman in lily foot slippers  ⟶

Several legends explain how the Chinese custom of keeping feet tiny began. One story goes back to ancient China. In this story an empress was born with small, deformed feet. Her father did not want his little girl shamed, so he told his court that only women with small feet would be thought pretty.

Foot-binding in China lasted hundreds of years. In 1902, however, Chinese law ordered that no child should suffer bound feet. Even then, the custom continued in secret until the 1930s.

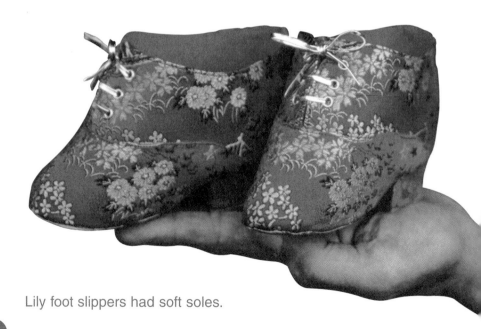

Lily foot slippers had soft soles.

Women have worn many other shoe styles that kept them from working and playing. Women in England made shoes called **mules** popular. Their mules were cloth slippers sewn with gold thread and metal lace. They usually fit the feet tightly. However, mules have no backs. What a sight to see women try to run in these!

Boots were a troublesome fashion in the 1800s because they had many buttons. Even worse, tiny feet were very popular. Women often wore boots that were much too small.

Sometimes a woman had to fasten more than 20 buttons on her boots just to go for a short walk!

# Chapter 4

# Shoes for Work and Play

Over several centuries many styles of boots became popular. Some boots helped people work and play. Shiny black "great boots" fit over softer shoes. Many had steel frames that supported leather uppers. They were worn much like galoshes are today. They could be worn anywhere and kept feet safe.

Pirates liked to wear high boots with wide tops. They used the extra space in their boot tops to hide stolen goods. Early Alaskan women found a different use for wide tops. They tucked their babies into their roomy deerskin boots to keep the babies warm.

This boot was worn in a battle more than 300 years ago.

Horseback riders often spent many days in the saddle. They found that strong, fitted boots protected them from rough horse hair. High boots are still the best foot covering for anyone who rides a horse. By the late 1800s, boots for men and women laced up. Active women, like men, discovered the value of wearing boots. Women wore boots to walk, to ride horseback, and to go out for the evening.

For a time buckles became a great fad in France. Shoes shone with brass and steel buckles. The rich wore silver and jeweled buckles on their shoes. Then the people of France revolted against their king and the rich nobles. Rich people no longer wanted to show off by wearing fancy shoes. Fancy buckles quickly went out of fashion.

Fancy buckles were often paired with fancy fabrics.

# Chapter 5

# Shoes Today

Before the 1300s most people made their shoes at home. Shoes were fitted by wrapping the foot with fabric or by drawing a pattern of the foot. Children usually wore smaller models of adult shoes. People with several children often made only one pair of children's shoes. This pair was made for the oldest child. When the shoes became too small, they were passed on to the next oldest child. Often the shoes fit poorly.

The inch was the idea of Edward II of England.

In the early 1300s, the king of England decided to use barley, a kind of grain, to measure things. A child's shoe that was 12 barleycorns long was size 12. He also decided that 3 barleycorns equaled 1 inch ($2\frac{1}{2}$ centimeters). Shoe sizes are still measured today in increases of $\frac{1}{3}$ inch.

A barleycorn measures about $\frac{1}{3}$ inch.

Today we use a machine to measure our feet.

Making shoes by hand was hard work.

Until the 1800s shoemakers shaped both shoes on one foot form. This meant that shoes fit on either foot, rather than having a right and a left shoe. Without a good fit, stiff leather rubbed the feet. This caused foot problems such as corns and broken bones. Shoemakers also built most shoes with simple hand tools. Even the best shoemaker could make only one pair of shoes a day. New shoes—both making them and wearing them—could be a giant pain!

In 1883 an American shoemaker invented a special machine. It shaped and sewed the shoe upper to the sole. The invention gave factories a way to make shoes of different sizes quickly and easily. Other machines cut pieces and stitched the upper parts and the soles of shoes. Factories could then produce more shoes in less time and at a lower cost.

Modern inventions have created different kinds of shoes and different ways of making them. Most shoes come from factories. Computers run many shoe factories. Shoes are designed on a computer and sewn by computer-controlled machines.

A modern shoe factory

Some shoes are still made from natural materials. Others are made of materials scientists created in test tubes, such as rubber. The discovery of rubber and how to use it led to one of the most popular shoe styles—athletic shoes. These were the first rubber-soled shoes. They had cloth uppers that laced up.

Athletic shoes were first worn for the lawn game of croquet (kroh KAY). But they cost $6. That was more than most people could afford. Then companies found ways to make the shoes for less money. Children especially liked them. One company renamed the shoes **sneakers** because they were quiet to wear.

People who ran schools liked the way sneakers left no marks on the floor. They began to require rubber-soled shoes for gym classes. With time, adults discovered the comfort and fit of rubber-soled shoes for everyday use, too.

During the past 40 years, athletic shoes have become a big business. Today's athletic shoes have many different kinds of uppers, many colors, and names of popular sports stars on them.

One company even decorates special sneakers with lace, pearls, and flowers for weddings. The bride wears her dressy high heels for the wedding. After the ceremony, she can slip on the soft wedding sneakers and enjoy her wedding party in comfort.

Athletic shoes come in hundreds of styles.

The next time you go out into the world, notice the many different kinds of athletic shoes people wear. Then look at the other kinds of shoes people wear. Chances are you'll see some new styles, along with sandals and boots and other styles that have been around for centuries.

# Glossary

**ancient** very old

**chopine** a raised shoe with a slipper on top of a platform

**clog** the English name for wooden shoes

**crakow** a pointy-toed shoe that was named for the Polish city of Krakow

**moccasin** a soft shoe that hugs the foot

**mule** a slipper that does not cover the heel of the foot

**patten** a rugged iron or wooden overshoe

**slipper** a shoe with a low upper that slips on

**sneaker** a rubber-soled shoe

**sole** the bottom part of a shoe that goes under the foot

**thong** an open sandal with a strap between two toes

**upper** the top part of a shoe that gives it shape

# Index